THIS COLLECTION
OF FAVORITE HYMNS

To: *Myrna*

From: *Don and Barb*

On the occasion of: *Christmas*

Date: *December 25, 2003*

About the Legacy of Helen Steiner Rice

Whatever the celebration, whatever the day, whatever the event, whatever the occasion, Helen Steiner Rice possessed the ability to express the appropriate feeling for that particular moment. Her positive attitude, her concern for others, and her love of God are identifiable threads woven into her life, her work . . . and even her death.

Prior to Mrs. Rice's passing, she established the Helen Steiner Rice Foundation, a nonprofit corporation that awards grants to worthy charitable programs assisting the elderly and the needy.

Royalties from the sale of this book will add to the financial capabilities of the Helen Steiner Rice Foundation. Because of limited resources, the foundation presently limits grants to qualified charitable programs in Lorain, Ohio, where Helen Steiner Rice was born, and Greater Cincinnati, Ohio, where Mrs. Rice lived and worked most of her life. Hopefully in the future, resources will be of sufficient size that broader geographical areas may be considered in the awarding of grants. Thank you for your assistance in helping to keep Helen's dream alive and growing.

Andrea R. Cornett, Administrator

AWAKE MY SOUL and SING

Poems Inspired by Favorite Hymns

HELEN STEINER RICE

stories and compilation by VIRGINIA J. RUEHLMANN

A HELEN STEINER RICE™ PRODUCT

Fleming H. Revell
A Division of Baker Book House Co
Grand Rapids, Michigan 49516

Dedicated
with praise, glory, and thanksgiving
to God, our Creator,
Jesus the Son,
and to the
Holy Spirit

© 2003 by Virginia J. Ruehlmann
and The Helen Steiner Rice™ Foundation

Published by Fleming H. Revell
a division of Baker Book House Company
P.O. Box 6287, Grand Rapids, MI 49516-6287

Printed in the United States of America

Library of Congress Cataloging-in-Publication Data is on file at the Library of Congress, Washington, D.C.

ISBN 0-8007-1846-1

The following have granted permission to reprint and record lyrics:
"How Great Thou Art" (p. 38) © 1953 Stuart K. Hine. Assigned to Manna Music, Inc., 35255 Brooten Rd., Pacific City, OR 97135. Renewed 1981. All rights reserved. Used by permission.

"Something Beautiful" (p. 64) © 1971 Gaither Music Company and "We Have This Moment Today" (p. 88) © 1975 Gaither Music Company, WJG, Inc., ASCAP. All rights controlled by Gaither Copyright Management. Used by permission.

"Surely the Presence of the Lord Is in This Place" (p. 66), words and music by Lanny Wolfe. © 1977 Lanny Wolfe Music, ASCAP. All rights controlled by Gaither Copyright Management. Used by permission.

"You Fill the Day" (p. 94), Joe Wise, composer. © 1968 GIA Publications, Inc. All rights reserved. Used with permission.

"The Lord's Prayer," Albert Hay Malotte, arranged by Carl Deiss, copyright 1935 by G. Schirmer, Inc., international copyright secured. Used by permission.

Conscientious efforts were made to locate owners of copyrighted materials and to secure proper permissions for inclusion in this book. If any error has been made, we apologize and on notification of such will make proper correction in subsequent printings.

CONTENTS

FOREWORD

All through my formative years our family had a lot of fun with music. Some of Mother's talent was passed along to all of us. My two brothers and I, as well as Mother and Father, spent a lot of time around the piano, harmonizing favorite songs and hymns.

In church, I loved sitting with my family, looking up at the stained glass windows and hearing the people around me sing hymns before my minister-father would give us his sermon each week. Church was the cornerstone of our family and our faith, and it was the center of almost every Christian community across the country in those days—the glue that held people together when times got hard. Hymns were our way of honoring and remembering all that God meant to us.

As the wife of the "minister to millions," Norman Vincent Peale, I have sat through innumerable services and witnessed the power of hymns to draw people together as one and set the mood for the pastor's message to be planted in each person's heart and mind.

Now we have the privilege of seeing together those timeless hymns of faith paired with the enduring poems of faith that Helen Steiner Rice loved to compose. Like the hymns themselves, Helen's lilting, tune-filled words have raised my spirits many times through the years. Her marvelous phrases are filled with truth and candor. Seeing them collected here, the "hymn poems" still strike a chord within my heart and express my deepest feelings in new, beautiful ways.

Let us sit down together, then, and enjoy anew the inspiring, tune-filled poems of Helen Steiner Rice alongside the familiar words of hymns that families have enjoyed for generations.

Ruth Stafford Peale
Pawling, New York

A Note on the Hymns

Make a joyful noise to the LORD, all the lands!
Serve the LORD with gladness!
Come into his presence with singing!

Psalm 100:1–2 RSV

Birds warble, brooks ripple, clouds float, trees sway, and animals join in with leaps and pirouettes. Is it any wonder that people must join in the earthly chorus in praise to God?

For thousands of years individuals have been inspired to compose lyrics and music in praise of God—hymns that are at once melodious, rhythmic, and symphonic.

Helen Steiner Rice added her voice to that chorus in a unique way. She loved the hymns and not only sang them but lived them, weaving them into her inspirational writings.

The title of this collection is taken from the hymn "Crown Him with Many Crowns" (p. 26). This collection features the poems inspired by Mrs. Rice's favorite age-old songs, along with the source lyrics and a nugget portion of background on how the hymn came to be in the first place. We imagine Mrs. Rice may have sung or hummed her way through these writings, as we hope you will do with the turn of each page. May the messages here ring with hope for you as they did for Helen Steiner Rice throughout life.

In praise of our Creator,
Virginia J. Ruehlmann

ALL CREATURES OF OUR GOD AND KING

All creatures of our God and King,
Lift up your voice and with us sing,
Alleluia! Alleluia!
Thou burning sun with golden beam,
Thou silver moon with softer gleam!
O praise Him, O praise Him,
Alleluia! Alleluia! Alleluia!

How the Hymn Came to Be

An Italian committed to a life of simplicity, service, and praise to God penned the words to "All Creatures of Our God and King." You might recognize the author as Saint Francis of Assisi, but he was born Giovanni Bernardone, the son of a wealthy nobleman.

Giovanni renounced his name and luxurious lifestyle at age twenty-five after encountering God in a church ruined by the war in which he had defended his city. In poverty Francis discovered the richness of God through his creation, which he reveled in the rest of his life. In 1225, as Francis was losing his eyesight, he expressed his appreciation for the beauty of God's gifts. He wrote *Canticle of the Sun*, including "All Creatures of Our God and King." William H. Draper (1855–1933), a rector in England, prepared the English translation of the hymn for a children's choir fair in the early 1900s, and in 1906 it made its first appearance in the *English Hymnal* in London.

You ask me how I know it's true that
   there is a living God.
A God who rules the universe — the
   sky, the sea, the sod —
A God who holds all creatures in the
   hollow of His hand,
A God who put infinity in one tiny
   grain of sand,
A God who made the seasons — winter,
   summer, fall and spring —
And put His flawless rhythm into each
   created thing,
A God who hangs the sun out slowly
   with the break of day
And gently takes the stars in and puts
   the night away,
A God whose mighty handiwork defies
   the skill of man,
For no architect can alter God's perfect
   master plan.
What better answers are there to prove
   His Holy Being
Than the wonders all around us that
   are ours just for the seeing?

ALL THINGS BRIGHT AND BEAUTIFUL

Each little flower that opens,
Each little bird that sings —
He made their glowing colors,
He made their tiny wings.

Refrain: All things bright and beautiful,
All creatures great and small,
All things wise and wonderful —
The Lord God made them all.

How the Hymn Came to Be

An Irish poet who gave all profits from her literary work to a school for deaf-mutes wrote these simple lyrics, put to the traditional English melody "Royal Oak" from *The Dancing Master* (1686).

Cecil Frances Humphreys Alexander (1818–1895) had begun writing at a very early age, and as a young woman, with her sister's help, founded the Girls Friendly Society for the deaf and mute in Londonderry, Northern Ireland. She published *Verses from the Scriptures* (1846) and *Hymns for Little Children* (1848), which includes "All Things Bright and Beautiful"—a song intended to explain to children the opening words of the Apostles' Creed. Cecil wrote more than four hundred hymns.

Each day at dawning,
 I lift my heart high
And raise up my eyes
 to the infinite sky.
I watch the night vanish
 as a new day is born,
And I hear the birds sing
 on the wings of the morn.
And as I give thanks
 I quietly pray,
"God, keep me and guide me
 and go with me today."

AMAZING GRACE

Amazing grace! How sweet the sound,
That saved a wretch like me!
I once was lost, but now am found,
Was blind, but now I see.

How the Hymn Came to Be

John Newton (1725–1807) knew the influence of a loving, faithful mother—and a loving, faithful God—as reflected in this beloved hymn. Newton penned the words to "Amazing Grace" after a violent storm at sea reminded him of amazing love.

Newton's mother had died when he was just seven; he adored her, and when his father remarried and sent Newton to a boarding school, the youth became rebellious and angry. He was soon known for profane living and eventually slave trading. But en route from Africa to England in 1748, fearing for his life as the ocean threatened to engulf his ship, Newton recalled Scripture taught by his mother. Soon after, he read *The Imitation of Christ* by Thomas à Kempis, and a spiritual transformation occurred.

Newton accepted Christ as his Savior and entered the ministry. At age thirty-nine, he was ordained an Anglican priest and was assigned to a church in Olney, a small factory town.

Newton coauthored with William Cowper one of England's earliest books of hymns, *The Olney Hymnal*. Included is "Amazing Grace," Newton's spiritual autobiography.

It's amazing and incredible, but it's as
 true as it can be,
God loves and understands us all, and
 that means you and me.
His grace is all-sufficient for both the
 young and old,
For the lonely and the timid, for the
 brash and for the bold.
His love knows no exceptions, so never
 feel excluded,
No matter who or what you are, your
 name has been included.
And no matter what your past has
 been, trust God to understand,
And no matter what your problem is,
 just place it in His hand.
For in all of our unloveliness this great
 God loves us still—
He loved us since the world began, and,
 what's more, He always will!

A MIGHTY FORTRESS IS OUR GOD

A mighty fortress is our God,
A bulwark never failing;
Our helper He amid the flood
Of mortal ills prevailing.
For still our ancient foe
Doth seek to work us woe;
His craft and pow'r are great,
And, armed with cruel hate,
On earth is not His equal.

How the Hymn Came to Be

For Martin Luther (1483–1546), a former Augustinian monk, accomplished musician, and active participant in the Reformation movement, music played an indispensable role in life and in worship. He maintained that God bestowed music as a generous gift to be shared. This conviction inspired his writing of both text and music for this hymn, which is frequently referred to as the "theme song of the Protestant Reformation." Luther's original version was written in German and later translated by Frederick H. Hedge (1805–1890).

Luther taught that in singing "A Mighty Fortress Is Our God" church members voice their love to the Almighty God, and through the enduring use of this hymn, congregations continue to do so. He based the message on several Scripture passages, such as 2 Samuel 22:1–3; Psalm 46; and Jeremiah 10:6–7.

God's love is like an island in life's
    ocean vast and wide —
A peaceful, quiet shelter from the rest-
    less, rising tide.
God's love is like an anchor when the
    angry billows roll —
A mooring in the storms of life, a
    stronghold for the soul.
God's love is like a fortress, and we
    seek protection there
When the waves of tribulation seem to
    drown us in despair.
God's love is like a harbor where our
    souls can find sweet rest
From the struggle and the tension of
    life's fast and futile quest.
God's love is like a beacon burning
    bright with faith and prayer;
And, through the changing scenes of
    life, we can find a haven there.

BATTLE HYMN OF THE REPUBLIC

Mine eyes have seen the glory of the coming of the Lord;
He is trampling out the vintage where the grapes of wrath are stored;
He hath loosed the fateful lightning of His terrible swift sword;
His truth is marching on.

Refrain: Glory! Glory! Hallelujah! Glory! Glory! Hallelujah!
Glory! Glory! Hallelujah! His truth is marching on.

How the Hymn Came to Be

Julia Ward Howe (1819–1910) arrived in Washington, D.C., in 1861 with her husband during the rising tensions of the Civil War. Soldiers crowded the streets, singing as they marched off to battle. Members of the Southern troops broke into the song "John Brown's Body," which told of the hanging of the abolitionist for his efforts to free slaves.

The song haunted Julia. A minister friend suggested she write new words for the music. That night she did, and she submitted the lyrics to James T. Fields, editor of the *Atlantic Monthly* magazine. Her "Battle Hymn of the Republic," set to the tune of a traditional American melody, was published in early 1862. Upon hearing the hymn the first time, President Lincoln asked that it be sung again, and it has—at inaugurations, funeral and memorial services, and for patriotic occasions ever since.

Give eternal rest to them, O Lord,
   whose souls have taken flight,
And lead them to a better world
   where there is peace and light.
Grant them eternal freedom
   from conflict, war and care,
And fulfill for them Thy prophecy —
   there shall be no night there.

SOLDIERS'

Hymn Book.

Compiled by
F. R. GOULDING
Macon, Ga.

MACON, GA.:
Boykin & Co.
1863

BLESSED ASSURANCE

Blessed assurance: Jesus is mine!
Oh, what a foretaste of glory divine!
Heir of salvation, purchase of God,
Born of His Spirit, washed in His blood.

Refrain: This is my story, this is my song,
Praising my Savior all the day long;
This is my story, this is my song,
Praising my Savior all the day long.

How the Hymn Came to Be

Of the more than 8,000 hymn texts written by Fanny J. Crosby, the song "Blessed Assurance" may have come most quickly. A personal friend, Phoebe Knapp (1839–1908), composed the music and played it for Crosby on a visit. "What message does the music send?" Knapp asked Crosby. Instantly Crosby replied, "Blessed assurance, Jesus is mine." With that response, the lyrics flowed.

Crosby (1820–1915) used a variety of pen names. This hymn, however, was never ascribed to another writer. In fact, when she died, her tombstone carried the words of the promise she had always claimed: "Blessed assurance: Jesus is mine! Oh, what a foretaste of glory divine!"

There are times when life overwhelms us
   and our trials seem too many to bear;
It is then we should stop to remember —
   God is standing by ready to share
The uncertain hours that confront us
   and fill us with fear and despair,
For God in His goodness has promised
   that the cross that He gives us to wear
Will never exceed our endurance
   or be more than our strength can bear;
And secure in that blessed assurance,
   we can smile as we face tomorrow,
For God holds the key to the future,
   and no sorrow or care we need borrow.

BLEST BE THE TIE THAT BINDS

Blest be the tie that binds
Our hearts in Christian love;
The fellowship of kindred minds
Is like to that above.

How the Hymn Came to Be

John Fawcett, orphaned at sixteen, longed for a sense of home. So in 1766, when he came to pastor a church in Wainsgate, England, he set about creating a family atmosphere. A strong friendship quickly developed between the pastor and his wife and their small congregation. While devotion and mutual esteem were abundant, monetary rewards were meager.

An opportunity came for Fawcett to succeed a well-known minister at a prosperous church in London. Wagons were loaded for the journey, and the parishioners who had gathered to bid farewell wept openly.

Fawcett and his wife could not leave. The wagons were unloaded, and Fawcett went back to work, but with a greater understanding of love. In one of his sermons he read an original poem titled "Brotherly Love."

Years later, that poem was set to the tune "Dennis," composed by Swiss music educator Hans (Johann) Georg Nägeli (1773–1836) and arranged by Lowell Mason (1792–1872), an American. "Blest Be the Tie That Binds" remains a testament to family and to John Fawcett, who served the same church for fifty years, declining many offers for more prestigious positions.

Friendship is a golden chain, the links
   are friends so dear,
And like a rare and precious jewel, it's
   treasured more each year.
It's clasped together firmly with a love
   that's deep and true,
And it's rich with happy memories and
   fond recollections, too.
Time can't destroy its beauty, for as
   long as memory lives,
Years can't erase the pleasure that the
   joy of friendship gives
For friendship is a priceless gift that
   can't be bought or sold,
And to have an understanding friend is
   worth far more than gold
And the golden chain of friendship is a
   strong and blessed tie
Binding kindred hearts together as the
   years go passing by.

BRIGHTEN THE CORNER

Do not wait until some deed of greatness you may do,
Do not wait to shed your light afar,
To the many duties ever near you now be true,
Brighten the corner where you are.

Refrain: Brighten the corner where you are!
Brighten the corner where you are!
Someone far from harbor you may guide across the bar;
Brighten the corner where you are!

How the Hymn Came to Be

Ina Mae Duley Ogdon was a busy wife and mother in Toledo, Ohio, in 1912, when her father suffered a severe stroke. For the next year she assumed, with her husband and their eleven-year-old son, full-time care of her father. It was a responsibility she accepted cheerfully, turning down invitations such as being a lecturer on the Chatauqua circuit.

Instead she focused on her family and wrote "Brighten the Corner," simple lyrics that she sent to her friend Charles H. Gabriel (1856–1932). At Mrs. Ogdon's request, Gabriel composed the music and sent the hymn to evangelist Billy Sunday's associate Homer Rodeheaver, who introduced "Brighten the Corner" in 1913 in Wilkes-Barre, Pennsylvania. By 1916 Theodore Roosevelt was using this tune at his political rallies.

Mrs. Ogdon died at age ninety-two, never fulfilling her dream of reaching people via the lecture circuit. However, her song lives on, encouraging all to work cheerfully wherever God has placed them.

We cannot all be famous or listed in
    "Who's Who,"
But every person, great or small, has
    important work to do.
For seldom do we realize the
    importance of small deeds
Or to what degree of greatness
    unnoticed kindness leads. . . .
So do not sit and idly wish for wider,
    new dimensions
Where you can put in practice your
    many good intentions,
But at the spot God placed you, begin
    at once to do
Little things to brighten up the lives
    surrounding you.
For if everybody brightened up the spot
    on which they're standing
By being more considerate and a
    little less demanding,
This dark old world would very soon
    eclipse the evening star,
If everybody brightened up the corner
    where they are.

Helen Steiner Rice

CHRIST THE LORD IS RISEN TODAY

Christ the Lord is risen today, Alleluia!
Sons of men and angels say: Alleluia!
Raise your joys and triumphs high, Alleluia!
Sing, ye heavens, and earth reply, Alleluia!

How the Hymn Came to Be

Charles Wesley (1707–1788) wrote "Christ the Lord Is Risen Today" to open the service in the first Wesleyan Chapel in London, England, in 1739, one year after his conversion while he was recovering from a recurring illness in a residence near St. Paul's Cathedral.

Moved by the compassion and care he received in Jesus' name, Wesley embarked on what was to be a lifelong pursuit of knowing and experiencing God more deeply and completely. In the process he wrote this hymn as the first of what would be six thousand to be sung in the chapel, or "Foundry Meeting House," he established.

The hymn is a lesson in resurrection—Jesus Christ's and ours with the assurance of life everlasting; the music is from the *Lyra Davidica* hymnal published in 1708. The actual composer was never identified nor was the editor who added the "alleluia" at the end of each line so that the words and tune balanced each other.

If there had never been a Christmas
    or the holy Christ Child's birth
Or the angels singing in the sky
    of promised peace on earth,
What would the world be like today
    with no eternal goal?
What would the temporal body be
    without a living soul?
Just what would give us courage
    to push on when hope is dead,
Except the Christmas message
    and the words our Father said—
"In love I send My only Son
    to live and die for you,
And through His resurrection,
    you will gain a new life, too."

CROWN HIM WITH MANY CROWNS

Crown Him with many crowns, the Lamb upon His throne,
Hark! how the heav'nly anthem drowns all music but its own!
Awake, my soul, and sing of Him who died for thee,
And hail Him as thy matchless King thru all eternity.

How the Hymn Came to Be

Inspired by Revelation 19:12, Matthew Bridges (1800–1894), a convert to Roman Catholicism from an Anglican background, wrote "Crown Him with Many Crowns." Originally titled "The Song of the Seraph," the hymn is an imaginative search for what the many crowns mentioned in Scripture might signify.

Thirty years after Bridges's penning of the lyrics, Godfrey Thring added six more stanzas to the original six. Each stanza exalts Jesus for a particular quality of His person and ministry.

Most hymnals today include four stanzas: three by Bridges and only one by Thring. The music is listed as "Diademata" (meaning "crowns" in Greek), by George J. Elvey (1816–1893), organist at St. George's Chapel in Windsor, England.

Before the dawn of Easter
There came Gethsemane.
Before the Resurrection
There were hours of agony.
For there can be no crown of stars
Without a cross to bear,
And there is no salvation
Without faith and love and prayer;
And when we take our needs to God
Let us pray as did His Son
That dark night in Gethsemane —
"Thy will, not mine, be done."

FAITH OF OUR FATHERS

Faith of our fathers! living still
In spite of dungeon, fire and sword;
O how our hearts beat high with joy
Whene'er we hear that glorious word!

Refrain: Faith of our fathers, holy faith!
We will be true to thee till death.

How the Hymn Came to Be

The Oxford Movement, whose members believed that a vital religious experience could be gained only through liturgy and ritual, strongly influenced minister-in-training Frederick William Faber (1814–1863). When Faber later converted to the Roman Catholic faith, he remembered and missed the movement's congregational singing of hymns. He concluded his life's assignment was to write hymns that emphasized the story and beliefs of the church.

By his death at age forty-nine, he had done just that, writing 150 such hymns, including "Faith of Our Fathers," a song that speaks of those who have suffered and died for their faith.

The melody, "St. Catherine's Tune," was composed by Henri Hemy (1818–1888) for an earlier hymn written in honor of Catherine of Alexander, a fourth-century martyr.

In 1874, the hymn took the shape by which most of us know it today when the refrain and first eight measures were added by James G. Walton (1821–1905). It has become a favorite of many; President Franklin D. Roosevelt particularly loved the hymn.

"Faith of our fathers," renew
   us again
And make us a nation of
   God-fearing men
Seeking Thy guidance, Thy love and
   Thy will,
For we are but pilgrims in search of
   Thee still.
And, gathered together on Thanksgiving
   Day,
May we lift up our hearts and our hands
   as we pray
To thank You for blessings we so little
   merit,
And grant us Thy love and teach us to
   share it.

FOR THE BEAUTY OF THE EARTH

For the beauty of the earth,
For the glory of the skies,
For the love which from our birth
Over and around us lies:
Christ our God, to Thee we raise
This our hymn of grateful praise.

How the Hymn Came to Be

Folliot Sanford Pierpoint (1835–1917), a teacher of the classics and an accomplished writer, journeyed back to historic Bath, England, one spring when he was twenty-nine. Struck by the beauty of his birthplace—the blue sky, green grass, and majestic Avon River meandering through flowering meadows—he penned the poem that became this well-known hymn.

Originally he titled his poem "The Sacrifice of Praise," intending that the hymn be sung for Communion services. It was a favorite for children as well as for the Thanksgiving season. The tune "Dix" was adapted by Conrad Kocher (1786–1872), a composer who played an integral role in reforming music in German churches.

"The earth is the Lord's, and the
   fullness thereof."
It speaks of His greatness —it sings
   of His love.
And each day at dawning, I lift my
   heart high
And raise up my eyes to the
   infinite sky.
I watch the night vanish as a new day
   is born,
And I hear the birds sing on the wings
   of the morn.
I see the dew glisten in crystal-like
   splendor
While God, with a touch that is
   gentle and tender;
Wraps up the night and softly tucks
   it away
And hangs out the sun to herald a
   new day
And so I give thanks and my heart
   kneels to pray,
"God, keep me and guide me and go
   with me today."

HIS EYE IS ON THE SPARROW

Why should I feel discouraged, Why should the shadows come,
Why should my heart be lonely and long for Heav'n and home,
When Jesus is my portion? My constant Friend is He;
His eye is on the sparrow, and I know He watches me,
His eye is on the sparrow, and I know He watches me.

How the Hymn Came to Be

For twenty years Mrs. Doolittle of Elmira, New York, was an invalid, cared for by her husband, a semi-invalid also confined to a wheelchair but determined to continue to work.

Often evangelists Dr. and Mrs. W. Stillman Martin visited the Doolittles, who seemed peaceful, content, and even cheerful. "How," Mrs. Martin once asked, "do you maintain such a positive outlook?"

Mrs. Doolittle replied that she did not worry because "His eye is on the sparrow, so I know He watches me."

The response kept ringing in Mrs. Martin's ears—and heart. Unable to dismiss it, she soon wrote her wheelchair-bound friend's response into a hymn. Dr. Martin composed the music, and the much-loved singer Ethel Waters introduced it during a Billy Graham crusade in Madison Square Garden in 1957.

God, give us eyes to see the beauty of
   the spring
And to behold Your majesty in every
   living thing,
And may we see in lacy leaves and
   every budding flower
The hand that rules the universe with
   gentleness and power
And may this lovely grandeur that
   spring lavishly imparts
Awaken faded flowers of faith lying
   dormant in our hearts
And give us ears to hear, dear God, the
   springtime song of birds,
With messages more meaningful than
   man's often empty words,
Telling harried human beings who are
   lost in dark despair;
"Be like us and do not worry, for God
   has you in His care."

HOLY, HOLY, HOLY

Holy, holy, holy! Lord God Almighty!
Early in the morning our song shall rise to Thee;
Holy, holy, holy! Merciful and mighty!
God in three persons, blessed Trinity!

How the Hymn Came to Be

An Anglican minister who couldn't find the right hymnal for his congregation set about to compile his own church songbook—and in the process wrote this majestic hymn. It was Reginald Heber's (1783–1826) frustrated attempts to find the *Olney Hymns* that also led him to organize his hymnal according to the church calendar, a first. He composed "Holy, Holy, Holy" for Trinity Sunday, which occurs eight weeks after Easter. The verse was put to the tune of John Bacchus Dykes's (1823–1876) "Nicaea," named for the Council of Nicaea, 325 A.D., when the Trinity was affirmed as a fundamental doctrine of the Christian faith.

When Heber died in 1826 at age forty-three, due to the stress of serving as Bishop of Calcutta in India, his widow published fifty-seven of her husband's hymns as a tribute to his memory and devoted ministry. "Holy, Holy, Holy" is from that collection.

There are many, many legends about
    St. Patrick's Day —
About the shamrock and the blarney
    and leprechauns at play,
The most delightful story is that God
    blessed the Emerald Isle
With the beauty of His goodness and
    the sunshine of His smile,
And how a dear, beloved Saint taught
    the Irish about God
Just by showing them a shamrock that
    was grown on Erin's sod.
He told them of the Trinity — the living
    Three in One —
The Holy Spirit, the Father, and His
    beloved Son.

Helen Steiner Rice

How Can I Keep from Singing?

My life flows on in endless song;
Above earth's lamentation,
I hear the sweet though far-off hymn
That hails a new creation.
Through all the tumult and the strife,
I hear the music ringing;
It finds an echo in my soul—
How can I keep from singing?

How the Hymn Came to Be

Though often mistaken for a traditional Shaker/Quaker hymn by recording artists like Pete Seeger, this inspiring Sunday school song was written by Robert Lowry just after the Civil War.

Lowry (1826–1899), who also wrote the beloved hymn "Shall We Gather at the River," published "How Can I Keep from Singing?" in *Bright Jewels for the Sunday School* (1869).

Ira Sankey (1840–1908), a Civil War veteran, later wrote an alternate tune to the song. During the war Sankey was known to help his unit chaplain by leading fellow soldiers in hymn singing. He became a gospel singer after the war and eventually came to the attention of evangelist Dwight L. Moody, whom he joined in leading revival meetings. One took place in October 1871, the evening of the Great Chicago Fire. Moody and Sankey barely escaped the blaze with their lives.

"The earth is the Lord's, and the
    fullness thereof . . ."
It speaks of his greatness and it sings
    of His love.
And the wonder and glory of the first
    Easter morn,
Like the first Christmas night when
    the Savior was born,
Are blended together in symphonic
    splendor.
And God, with a voice that is gentle
    and tender;
Speaks to all hearts attuned to
    His voice,
Bidding His listeners to gladly rejoice,
For He that was born to be crucified
Arose from the grave to be glorified.
And the birds in the trees and the
    flowers of spring
All join in proclaiming this
    heavenly King.

HOW GREAT THOU ART

O Lord my God, when I in awesome wonder
Consider all the worlds° Thy hands have made,
I see the stars, I hear the rolling° thunder,
Thy pow'r thro'out the universe displayed.

Refrain: Then sings my soul, my Savior God, to Thee:
How great Thou art, how great Thou art!

How the Hymn Came to Be

As layers of work make a masterpiece painting, several events and individuals contributed to this hymn. The first contributor was a Swedish preacher stunned by the beauty of his homeland. Carl Boberg (1859–1940) composed a poem titled "O Store Gud" ("O Great God"), which was published in 1886 with the refrain "Then doth my soul burst forth in song of praise, Oh, great God." Several years later, Boberg heard his poem sung to a traditional Swedish tune.

Manfred von Glehn next translated Boberg's version into German and supplied the name "Wie gross bist Du."

The beauty of a countryside inspired another version of the song in the 1920s, when English missionaries Reverend and Mrs. Stuart Hine were serving in Russia. A thunderstorm caught them by surprise, and nature staged a spectacular fireworks display. When the sun reappeared and birds started singing, Stuart Hine wrote three verses of a poem expressing adoration to God. He called the poem "How Great Thou Art" and set it to the Swedish folk melody he'd learned in Russia. He later added a fourth stanza.

*Author's original words are *works* and *mighty*.

*God is so lavish in all that He's done
To make this great world such a
    wonderful one—
His mountains are high, His oceans
    are deep,
And vast and unmeasured the prairie
    lands sweep.
His heavens are dotted with
    uncounted jewels,
For joy without measure is one
    of God's rules.*

Helen Steiner Rice

I Love to Tell the Story

I love to tell the story of unseen things above,
Of Jesus and His glory, of Jesus and His love;
I love to tell the story because I know 'tis true;
It satisfies my longings as nothing else can do.

Refrain: I love to tell the story! 'Twill be my
  theme in glory
To tell the old, old story of Jesus and His love.

Tell Me the Old, Old, Story

Tell me the old, old story of unseen things
  above,
Of Jesus and His glory, of Jesus and His love.
Tell me the story simply, as to a little child,
For I am weak and weary, and helpless and
  defiled.

Refrain: Tell me the old, old story!
Tell me the old, old story!
Tell me the old, old story
Of Jesus and His love.

How the Hymns Came to Be

*T*elling others about her Savior was one of thirty-year-old Katherine Hankey's greatest joys. Hankey (1834–1911), a member of a well-to-do English family, gained a reputation for her famous London Bible stories. So when illness forced her to rest for one year, she poured her convictions into writing about the work she loved.

A lengthy poem called "The Story Told" resulted—with one hundred verses divided into two sections. "I Love to Tell the Story" came from the second section and "Tell Me the Old, Old Story" from the first.

Initially Hankey created her own music for each hymn, but in 1867 well-known composer William H. Doane put each hymn to a different musical setting.

Eight years later, William G. Fischer (1835–1912), a Philadelphia music professor, added the now famous refrain to "I Love to Tell the Story" and composed the tune familiar today.

They asked me how I know it's true
That the Savior lived and died.
And if I believe the story
That the Lord was crucified.
And I have so many answers
To prove His Holy Being,
Answers that are everywhere
Within the realm of seeing.
The leaves that fell at autumn
And were buried in the sod
Now budding on the tree boughs
To lift their arms to God.
The flowers that were covered
And entombed beneath the snow
Pushing through the darkness
To bid the spring "hello."
On every side, great nature
Retells the old, old story
So who am I to question
The Resurrection Glory.

I NEED THEE EVERY HOUR

I need Thee every hour, most gracious Lord;
No tender voice like Thine can peace afford.

Refrain: I need Thee, O I need Thee;
Every hour I need Thee;
O bless me now, my Savior,
I come to Thee.

How the Hymn Came to Be

Annie Sherwood Hawks (1835–1918), a wife and a mother of three, wrote the words to this hymn in her late thirties. One morning while doing chores, Hawks experienced a profound sensation of closeness to the Lord. She wondered how anyone at any time in any situation could endure life without belief in and love for Jesus. Serenity and peace came over her, and the message "I need Thee every hour" traveled through her mind. She sat down, wrote the lyrics, and later showed them to her pastor, Robert Lowry. He in turn wrote the tune and the refrain. The hymn was published and heard for the first time in Cincinnati, Ohio, at the National Baptist Sunday School Convention in 1872.

Dr. Robert Lowry (1826–1899) was a musically talented pastor who was dedicated to preaching the word of God, having given his heart and life to Christ when he was seventeen.

No one ever sought the Father and
   found He was not there,
And no burden is too heavy to be
   lightened by a prayer.
No problem is too intricate, and no
   sorrow that we face
Is too deep and devastating to be
   softened by His grace. . . .
And men of every color, every race
   and every creed
Have but to seek the Father in their
   deepest hour of need.
God asks for no credentials — He
   accepts us with our flaws.
He is kind and understanding and
   He welcomes us because
We are His erring children and He
   loves us, every one,
And He freely and completely
   forgives all that we have done,
Asking only if we're ready to follow
   where He leads,
Content that in His wisdom He will
   answer all our needs.

Helen Steiner Rice

IT IS WELL WITH MY SOUL

When peace, like a river, attendeth my way,
When sorrows like sea-billows roll;
Whatever my lot, Thou hast taught me to say,
"It is well, it is well with my soul."

How the Hymn Came to Be

In 1871 Horatio G. Spafford (1828–1888), an attorney in Chicago, his wife, and their four daughters mourned when the family's only son died. Three years later they lost most of their personal belongings in the Great Chicago Fire. But neither of these tragedies could prepare them for what was to come later that year.

Anna Spafford and the four girls sailed for England on the French steamship *Ville de Havre*. Off the coast of Ireland, however, it collided with another vessel and sank; among those who drowned were the four Spafford daughters.

Mrs. Spafford cabled her husband two words: "Saved alone." He departed for England to comfort his wife. On board he gained inner strength by reading his Bible. As the ship passed the spot where his four daughters had drowned, Spafford composed the emotional poem "It Is Well with My Soul."

Remarkably, Spafford's friend Philip Bliss (1838–1876), who composed the tune "Ville du Havre" for this hymn, also suffered tragedy. He and his wife lost their lives in a train accident. But Bliss's music, like Spafford's unfailing words of faith, lives on.

We know we must pass through the
seasons God sends,
Content in the knowledge that
everything ends,
And, oh, what a blessing to know there
are reasons
And to find that our souls must, too, have
their seasons —
Bounteous seasons and barren
ones, too,
Times for rejoicing and times to
be blue —
But meeting these seasons of dark
desolation
With the strength that is born of
anticipation
Comes from knowing that every
season of sadness
Will surely be followed by a springtime
of gladness.

Helen Steiner Rice

JESUS LOVES ME

Jesus loves me! this I know,
For the Bible tells me so;
Little ones to Him belong,
They are weak but He is strong.

How the Hymn Came to Be

Anna Warner (1820–1915), her sister, Susan, and their father resided at *Good Crag*, a lovely home near West Point Military Academy. For many years the two sisters conducted weekly Bible classes for the cadets.

When the elder Warner passed away in 1860, the sisters decided to augment their income with more serious literary endeavors. They worked together on a novel, *Say and Seal*, Susan writing the text and Anna composing a poem used to comfort a dying child in the story. Dr. William Bradbury, noted teacher and music publisher, composed the melody for Anna's poem and added the well-known chorus.

Following the demise of Anna and Susan, *Good Crag* was willed to West Point and became a national shrine. The sisters were accorded burial with military honors in testimony of the roles they played in enhancing the spiritual lives of young cadets.

"Jesus loves me, this I know, for the Bible
   tells me so."
Little children ask no more, for love is all
   they're looking for,
And in a small child's shining eyes the
   faith of all the ages lies.
And tiny hands and tousled heads that
   kneel in prayer by little beds
Are closer to the dear Lord's heart and of
   His kingdom more a part
Than we who search and never find the
   answers to our questioning minds . . .
And the more man learns, the less he
   knows and the more involved his
   thinking grows,
And in his arrogance and pride, no
   longer is man satisfied
To place his confidence and love with
   childlike faith in God above.
Oh heavenly Father, grant again a simple,
   childlike faith to men,
And with a small child's trusting eyes,
   may all men come to realize
That faith alone can save man's soul and
   lead him to a higher goal.

JOYFUL, JOYFUL WE ADORE THEE

Joyful, joyful, we adore Thee, God of glory, Lord of love;
Hearts unfold like flowers before Thee, hail Thee, as the sun above.
Melt the clouds of sin and sadness, drive the dark of doubt away;
Giver of immortal gladness, fill us with the light of day!

How the Hymn Came to Be

Enthralled with the beauty of the Berkshire Mountains while guest preaching at Williams College in Massachusetts, scholar, minister, and author Henry Van Dyke wrote the words for "Joyful, Joyful We Adore Thee" as a poem in 1911.

Van Dyke (1852–1933), known for inspirational classics such as *The Other Wiseman*, requested that the poem be sung to "Hymn of Joy" from Beethoven's Ninth Symphony. Inspiration for Beethoven's symphony came from "Ode to Joy," a work of his poet friend Friedrich Schiller (1759–1805).

In addition to being a prolific writer of devotional and literary material, Van Dyke was also the pastor of Brick Presbyterian Church in New York City, a professor of English literature at Princeton University, a Navy chaplain in World War I, and an American ambassador to Holland and Luxembourg (appointed by President Wilson). Despite all his achievements in libraries and the classroom, he wrote, "nothing can compare to the glories in the nature created by our God."

Only what we give away
Enriches us from day to day,
For not in getting but in giving
Is found the lasting joy of living.
For no one ever had a part
In sharing treasures of the heart
Who did not feel the impact of
The magic mystery of God's love.
And love alone can make us kind
And give us joy and peace of mind,
So live with joy unselfishly
And you'll be blessed abundantly.

JOY TO THE WORLD

Joy to the world! the Lord is come.
Let earth receive her King;
Let every heart prepare Him room,
And heaven and nature sing,
And heaven and nature sing,
And heaven, and heaven and nature sing.

O HOLY NIGHT

O Holy Night! the stars are brightly
    shining,
It is the night of the dear Savior's birth;
Long lay the world in sin and error pining,
Till He appeared and the soul felt its worth.
A thrill of hope the weary world rejoices,
For yonder breaks a new and glorious
    morn;
Fall on your knees, Oh, hear the angel
    voices!
O night divine, O night when Christ was
    born!
O night, O holy night, O night divine!

How the Hymns Came to Be

Always fond of Psalm 100, which begins "Make a joyful noise to the Lord," Calvinist pastor Isaac Watts composed "Joy to the World." Watts (1674–1748) took his poem to Lowell Mason (1792–1872), who set it to his arrangement of "Antioch," music originally composed by George Frederick Handel.

Placide Clappeau, a wine merchant and mayor of Roquemaure, France, wrote the poem "O Holy Night" in 1847. It was translated into English by John S. Dwight (1812–1893), who was a graduate of Harvard University and Cambridge Theological College. The music, titled "Cantique de Noel," was composed by Adolphe C. Adam (1803–1856).

Christmas is more than a day
    at the end of the year,
More than a season of joy
    and good cheer —
Christmas is really God's pattern
    for living
To be followed all year by unselfish
    giving.
For if we lived Christmas each day,
    as we should,
And made it our aim to always do
    good,
We'd find the lost key to meaningful
    living
That comes not from getting, but
    from unselfish giving.

JUST A CLOSER WALK WITH THEE

I am weak, but Thou art strong;
Jesus, keep me from all wrong;
I'll be satisfied as long
As I walk, let me walk close to Thee.

Refrain: Just a closer walk with Thee,
Grant it, Jesus, is my plea,
Daily walking close to Thee,
Let it be, dear Lord, let it be.

How the Hymn Came to Be

Some of our most touching hymns are those that have been passed down from life on Southern plantations. Fortunately the songs have withstood the long journey; unfortunately the names of the authors and composers have not. Several are identified as "Anonymous" or "Author Unknown," and the music is noted as "American Folk Song." These hymns often tell a story, express deep emotions, use a question and response format, and are—as they are frequently classified—deeply spiritual.

Good morning, God!
You are ushering in another day,
  untouched and freshly new,
So here I am to ask You, God,
  if You'll renew me, too.
Forgive the many errors
  that I made yesterday
And let me try again, dear God,
  to walk closer in Thy way.
But, Father, I am well aware
I can't make it on my own,
So take my hand and hold it tight,
  for I can't walk alone.

LEANING ON THE EVERLASTING ARMS

What a fellowship, what a joy divine,
Leaning on the everlasting arms;
What a blessedness, what a peace is mine,
Leaning on the everlasting arms.

Refrain: Leaning, leaning, safe and secure from all alarms;
Leaning, leaning, leaning on the everlasting arms.

How the Hymn Came to Be

Anthony J. Showalter (1858–1924), well known for his expertise in the Singing School Movement in the late 1880s, had just returned home to Alabama from coaching a hymn class in South Carolina when he learned that two of his students had each just lost a wife to death.

Showalter was stunned and immediately sent his sympathies, quoting Deuteronomy 33:27. Yet the message that "the eternal God is your dwelling place, and underneath are the everlasting arms" stuck with him. He decided to put this idea into song. Composing a basic melody, he quickly crafted a refrain that worked, but he felt unhappy with the final stanzas he attempted.

Showalter consulted Elisha Hoffman (1839–1929), a fellow poet and lyricist, who added three stanzas, completing the hymn.

Sometimes we feel uncertain and
   unsure of everything—
Afraid to make decisions, dreading
   what the day will bring.
We keep wishing it were possible to
   dispel all fear and doubt
And to understand more readily just
   what life is all about.
God has given us the answers, which
   too often go unheeded,
But if we search His promises we'll
   find every thing that's needed
To lift our faltering spirits and renew
   our courage, too,
For there's absolutely nothing too
   much for God to do.
For the Lord is our salvation and our
   strength in every fight,
Our redeemer and protector, our eter-
   nal guiding light.
He has promised to sustain us, He's
   our refuge from all harms,
And underneath this refuge are the
   everlasting arms.

LOVE DIVINE, ALL LOVES EXCELLING

Love divine, all loves excelling, joy of heav'n to
    earth come down;
Fix in us Thy humble dwelling; all Thy faithful
    mercies crown.
Jesus, Thou art all compassion, pure,
    unbounded love Thou art;
Visit us with Thy salvation; enter ev'ry
    trembling heart.

HARK! THE HERALD ANGELS SING

Hark! the herald angels sing,
"Glory to the newborn King;
Peace on earth, and mercy mild,
God and sinners reconciled!"
Joyful, all ye nations, rise,
Join the triumph of the skies;
With th' angelic host proclaim,
"Christ is born in Bethlehem!"

Refrain: Hark! the herald angels sing
"Glory to the newborn King."

How the Hymns Came to Be

Frequently cited as the "poet and soul of Methodism," Charles Wesley (1707–1788) composed these hymns and others, such as "Christ the Lord Is Risen Today," to teach Christian doctrines.

He intended the various verses of "Love Divine, All Loves Excelling" to be instructional on topics such as the birth of Christ, victory over sin, the presence of the Holy Spirit in one's life, and life after death. Set to the tune "Beecher" by John Zundel (1815–1882), it is used in many denominations and presents Christ's grace and mercy to all.

In 1739 Wesley wrote the lyrics to "Hark! the Herald Angels Sing," though not with the melody with which we're familiar. In 1855 William Cummings (1831–1915) combined Wesley's lyrics with a melody written by Felix Mendelssohn. Wesley's original lyrics have been altered through the years.

"Love divine, all loves excelling,"
Make my humbled heart Your dwelling
For without Your love divine,
Total darkness would be mine.
My earthly load I could not bear
If You were not there to share
All the pain, despair and sorrow
That almost make me dread tomorrow,
For I am often weak and weary,
And life is dark and bleak and dreary
But somehow when I realize
That He who made the sea and skies
And holds the whole world in His hand
Has my small soul in His command,
It gives me strength to try once more
To somehow reach the heavenly door
Where I will live forevermore
With friends and loved ones I adore.

PRAISE GOD, FROM WHOM ALL BLESSINGS FLOW

Praise God, from whom all blessings flow;
Praise Him all creatures here below;
Praise Him above, ye heavenly host;
Praise Father, Son and Holy Ghost.

How the Hymn Came to Be

For such a simple hymn, its writer and story took a long, circuitous route. Thomas Ken, a chaplain to three European kings in the early 1600s, penned the words. Ken was a Winchester College scholar from Oxford University. Orphaned at an early age, he was raised by his older sister and her husband, Izaak Walton, who sent him to Winchester. Ken was ordained a minister in the Church of England at age twenty-five. As the English chaplain at the royal court at the Hague, he criticized the behavior of those in control in the Dutch capital. He was required to return to England where Charles II appointed him as one of his personal chaplains and later Bishop of Bath and Wells.

French-born Louis Bourgeois moved to Switzerland in 1540, became involved with the Reformed Reformation Movement, and was given the assignment of providing melodies for the metrical psalms to be in the *Genevan Psalter*. The tune "Old Hundredth" used for Ken's "Praise God, from Whom All Blessings Flow," also known as "The Doxology," was adapted by Bourgeois.

Thank You, God, for everything—
   the big things and the small—
For every good gift comes from God,
   the Giver of them all,
And all too often we accept without any
   thanks or praise
The gifts God sends as blessings each
   day in many ways.
And so at this Thanksgiving time we
   offer up a prayer
To thank You, God, for giving us a lot
   more than our share. . . .
Oh, make us more aware, dear God, of
   little daily graces
That come to us with sweet surprise
   from never-dreamed-of places.
Then thank You for the miracles we are
   much too blind to see,
And give us new awareness of our
   many gifts from Thee.
And help us to remember that the key
   to life and living
Is to make each prayer a prayer of thanks
And every day a day of thanksgiving.

ROCK OF AGES

Rock of Ages, cleft for me, let me hide myself in Thee;
Let the water and the blood, from Thy wounded side which flowed,
Be of sin the double cure, save me from its guilt and pow'r.

How the Hymn Came to Be

An Anglican, passionate to prove that the cross of Christ is the source of salvation and not a person's own efforts, wrote "Rock of Ages." Ordained into the ministry of the Church of England in 1762, Augustus Montague Toplady (1740–1778) passionately disagreed with the Wesleys, whom he debated frequently and publicly.

As an ideal culmination for his published commentary, Toplady wrote an article for *The Gospel Magazine* in 1776, as well as this new hymn which was originally titled "A Living and Dying Prayer for the Holiest Believer in the World."

Thomas Hastings (1784–1872), born in America, composed the music for Toplady's famous hymn in 1830. As a well-recognized musician, despite his limited formal training, Hastings has been identified as instrumental to the growth and progress of church music in the United States. Though he suffered vision difficulties his entire life, he completed more than fifty collections of religious music, including more than 1,500 original hymn tunes and spiritual lyrics.

It's easy to say "In God we trust"
   when life is radiant and fair;
But the test of faith is only found
   when there are burdens to bear.
For our claim to faith in the sunshine
   is really no faith at all,
For when roads are smooth and days
     are bright
   our need for God is so small.
And no one discovers the fullness
   or the greatness of God's love
Unless they have walked in the darkness
   with only a light from above.
For the faith to endure whatever comes
   is born of sorrow and trials
And strengthened only by discipline
   and nurtured by self-denials.
So be not disheartened by troubles,
   for trials are the building blocks,
On which to erect a fortress of faith,
   secure on God's ageless rocks.

SOFTLY AND TENDERLY

Softly and tenderly Jesus is calling,
Calling for you and for me;
See on the portals He's waiting and watching,
Watching for you and for me.

Refrain: Come home, come home,
Ye who are weary, come home;
Earnestly, tenderly, Jesus is calling—
Calling, "O sinner, come home!"

How the Hymn Came to Be

An Ohio legislator's son, who owned and managed his own publishing and music store, penned the words and music of "Softly and Tenderly."

Will L. Thompson was schooled in Boston Music School (1870–1873), instructed in advanced music theory in Germany, and enjoyed a flourishing career writing secular songs before composing this hymn. He enjoyed financial success, but it wasn't enough.

Thompson wanted to compose gospel hymns for the populace. He began to do this and soon was traveling via horse and buggy to different areas throughout the Buckeye State to sing his songs to members of communities everywhere.

Silently the green leaves grow,
In silence falls the soft, white snow,
Silently the flowers bloom,
In silence sunshine fills a room —
Silently bright stars appear;
In silence velvet night draws near,
And silently God enters in
To free a troubled heart from sin.
For God works silently in lives,
For nothing spiritual survives
Amid the din of a noisy street
Where raucous crowds with hurrying feet
And blinded eyes and deafened ears
Are never privileged to hear
The message God wants to impart
To every troubled, weary heart.
For only in a quiet place
Can one behold God face to face.

Helen Steiner Rice

SOMETHING BEAUTIFUL

Something beautiful, something good
All my confusion He understood
All I had to offer Him was brokenness and strife,
But He made something beautiful of my life.

How the Hymn Came to Be

Gloria Gaither was soothing her three-year-old daughter Suzanne over a ruined finger painting project when the words to this hymn came to her.

"Oh, Mommy," Suzanne had sobbed. "I tried to make you something beautiful, but just look! I dropped some paint." Thinking the project was ruined, Suzanne was to learn a very important lesson of life: If one keeps the faith, something beautiful can be restored.

Gloria wiped away her toddler's tears, cuddled her, then gave her a clean sheet of art paper, and in a display of how God works in the souls of men and women, little Suzanne did create something beautiful! Beyond what she could have imagined came this beautiful song, published in 1971, with lyrics penned by Gloria and music written by her husband, Bill.

Often your tasks will be many and
    more than you think you can do.
Often the road will be rugged, and the
    hills insurmountable, too.
But always remember, the hills ahead
    are never as steep as they seem,
And with faith in your heart, start
    upward and climb till you reach
    your dream.
For nothing in life that is worthy is ever
    too hard to achieve
If you have the courage to try it and you
    have the faith to believe.
For faith is a force that is greater than
    knowledge or power or skill,
And many defeats turn to triumphs if
    you trust in God's wisdom and will.
For faith is a mover of mountains —
    there's nothing that God cannot do —
So start out today with faith in your
    heart and climb till your dream
    comes true.

SURELY THE PRESENCE OF THE LORD IS IN THIS PLACE

Surely the presence of the Lord is in this place
I can feel His mighty power and His grace;
I can hear the brush of angels' wings,
I see glory on each face.
Surely the presence of the Lord is in this place.

How the Hymn Came to Be

As Lanny Wolfe and his trio waited to be announced at the dedication of a new church in Columbia, Mississippi, this hymn came to him. The church officers, public officials, program participants, and members of the congregation watched as Wolfe stepped immediately to the piano, sat down, and played the inspired tune. Quickly he taught the lyrics to the audience and the other members of the trio.

Nothing has been altered in the hymn since that initial rendition. The scrap of paper on which Lanny Wolfe sketched a few notes and words before taking the stage is now framed and hangs in the entrance of that church in Mississippi.

"God doesn't live in church walls or in stained glass," Wolfe later remarked. "God lives in the praise of people, and so we need to be reminded where God lives and without God's presence, all is in vain. We can meet God in a brush arbor, at an altar of prayer in a field, under a tree, in our bedroom, or in a sanctuary. God is omnipresent. He is everywhere."

I have prayed on my knees in the morn-
    ing, I have prayed as I walked along,
I have prayed in the silence and dark-
    ness, and I've prayed to the tune of a
    song. . . .
I have prayed in churches and chapels,
    cathedrals and synagogues, too,
But often I had the feeling that my
    prayers were not getting through.
And I realized then that our Father is not
    really concerned where we pray
Or impressed by our manner of worship
    or the eloquent words that we say.
He is only concerned with our feelings,
    and He looks deep into our hearts
And hears the cry of our souls' deep need
    that no words could ever impart.
So it isn't the prayer that's expressive or
    offered in some special spot —
It's the sincere plea of a sinner, and God
    can tell whether or not
We honestly seek His forgiveness and
    earnestly mean what we say,
And then and then only God answers the
    prayers that we fervently pray.

SWEET HOUR OF PRAYER

Sweet hour of prayer, sweet hour of prayer,
That calls me from a world of care,
And bids me at my Father's throne
Make all my wants and wishes known:
In seasons of distress and grief
My soul has often found relief,
And oft escaped the tempter's snare
By thy return, sweet hour of prayer.

How the Hymn Came to Be

A mystery surrounds who truly wrote the words to this beloved hymn, which was first published as a poem in The New York Observer, September 13, 1845. At first it was believed that a blind preacher in Coleshill, England, composed the words, which he recited to Thomas Salmon, his pastor. Visiting the States, Salmon had shown the poem to an editor at the Observer, but the source of the poem was never validated.

In fact, a blind preacher did minister in Coleshill at the time, but a minister by the name printed with the poem in the *Observer*—William W. Walford (1772–1850)—also lived at that time in nearby Homerton. Walford had authored many books, one of which centered on prayer and embodied the thoughts and expressions in "Sweet Hour of Prayer."

William B. Bradbury (1816–1868), a distinguished composer and manufacturer of pianos, created the tune "Sweet Hour" in 1861.

Dear God, much too often we seek You
    in prayer
Because we are wallowing in our own
    self-despair.
We make every word we lamentingly
    speak
An imperative plea for whatever we seek.
We pray for ourselves and so seldom for
    others —
We're concerned with our problems and
    not with our brothers.
We seem to forget, Lord, that the sweet
    hour of prayer
Is not for self-seeking but to place in
    Your care
All the lost souls, unloved and unknown,
And to keep praying for them until
    they're Your own.
For it's never enough to seek God
    i̶n̶...
W̶e̶...̶ ̶ ̶r̶s̶ who are lost

S̶o̶...̶t̶ the power

I̶s̶...̶ ̶the world in
    ...

TAKE MY LIFE, AND LET IT BE

Take my life and let it be consecrated, Lord, to Thee;
Take my hands and let them move at the impulse of Thy love,
At the impulse of Thy love.

How the Hymn Came to Be

Frances Ridley Havergal had an enormous desire to bring others to Christ. In 1874, she visited a home in London where several others were also guests. She learned that some were unbelievers and others struggled with doubts. During her stay she prayed for each one to see God's love. Soon she sensed her prayers had been answered; her final night in London she was so excited about the changes in her new friends that she could not sleep. She sat up and wrote the words to the hymn, "Take My Life, and Let It Be."

Just four years after Frances wrote the text, it was published as a hymn to the tune "Hendon," named for a steep cliff near St. Paul's Cathedral in London, and composed by Henri A. Ce'sar Malan (1787–1864), a Swiss evangelist and creator of more than 1,000 melodies.

At age forty-two, Havergal died. She had struggled all her life with illness but had yielded herself completely to Christ, writing many hymns and memorizing the Psalms and much of the New Testament at even a young age. She was proficient in Latin, Hebrew, Greek, French, and German—all of which carry translations of this beautiful hymn.

Take me and break me and make me,
　　dear God,
　　just what You want me to be.
Give me the strength to accept what You send
　　and eyes with the vision to see
All the small, arrogant ways that I have
　　and the vain little things that I do.
Make me aware that I'm often concerned
　　more with myself than with You.
Uncover before me my weakness and greed
　　and help me to search deep inside
So I may discover how easy it is
　　to be selfishly lost in my pride.
And then in Thy goodness and mercy,
　　look down on this weak, erring one
And tell me that I am forgiven
　　for all I've so willfully done,
And teach me to humbly start following
　　the path that the dear Savior trod
So I'll find at the end of life's journey
　　a home in the city of God.

TELL ME THE STORY OF JESUS

Tell me the story of Jesus,
Write on my heart every word,
Tell me the story most precious,
Sweetest that ever was heard.

How the Hymn Came to Be

When you know that the woman who penned this hymn had been blinded in infancy, the ideas in "Tell Me the Story of Jesus" take on an obvious significance.

Fanny Crosby lost her sight when six weeks old because of a warm poultice applied to her infected eyes. Throughout her life, she treasured the times others would read to her from Scripture or tell of Jesus in their lives. She relied greatly on such communication, though she was an accomplished scholar of the New York City Institute for the Blind. She went to the school at age eleven as a pupil and stayed for twenty-three years, leaving as a teacher.

Many of her poems, such as "Tell Me the Story of Jesus" and "All the Way My Savior Leads Me," draw upon realities Fanny Crosby understood well—relying on the radiance of Jesus for guidance.

The earnestness, simplicity, and strong scriptural basis of Fanny's poetry keeps her songs among the best-learned and loved. It also makes her one of the most prolific songwriters, as beginning in her early forties she was under contract for several years to furnish her publishers with three hymns every week. Faithfully, she completed more than 8,000 songs, and her work continues to fill hymnals and be sung, even today.

God, make us aware
   that the Savior died—
Was nailed to a cross
   and was crucified—
Not to redeem
   just a chosen few
But to save all who ask
   for forgiveness from You.

THE CHURCH IN THE WILDWOOD

There's a church in the valley by the wildwood
No lovelier spot in the dale;
No place is so dear to my childhood
As the little brown church in the vale.

How the Hymn Came to Be

William Savage Pitts was traveling by stagecoach from Chicago to his fiancée's home in Fredericksburg, Iowa, when the coach stopped at Bradford, Iowa, to rest and water the horses. Pitts took advantage of this opportunity to admire the picturesque Cedar River Valley.

Gazing from the top of a hill at a grove of trees clustered in the valley below, Pitts announced to a fellow passenger that this was the perfect setting for a church—and furthermore it should be named "The Little Brown Church in the Vale."

The image stuck with him long after he returned to his medical studies at Chicago's School of Medicine. One night in 1857, Pitts composed the verses and music of the hymn. After completing medical school, he returned to Fredericksburg to establish his practice. Dr. Pitts, gifted in music, also founded music and singing schools in the area.

When he learned that a church was being built at the very spot he had envisioned years earlier, Pitts rummaged through his papers for the song he'd written as a bachelor. The building was ready for dedication in the winter of 1864, as was Pitts, who sang his original musical work.

I sat among the people in the church
    of my childhood and youth.
I came back to sing the songs of praise
    and hear the words of truth.
I looked into the faces of the young
    folks and the old
And listened, as I used to, to the
    sweetest story ever told.
I had come back home to visit and
    meet friends in glad reunion,
But the Sunday that I went to church
    turned out to be communion,
And so it was when I arose from my
    communion prayer
I no longer saw just faces, for God
    was standing there.

THE LORD'S MY SHEPHERD

The Lord's my Shepherd, I'll not want.
He makes me down to lie
In pastures green; He leadeth me
The quiet waters by.

How the Hymn Came to Be

*D*irect from Scripture, the text of this hymn reaches out to the lonely, which is why gifted writers and composers through the ages have crafted so many variations.

Francis Rous, speaker of the Supreme Authority of the Commonwealth of England in 1653 (which declared itself Parliament and then dissolved itself), wrote one version of the song for the *Scottish Psalter* in 1650. In 1812 William Gardiner (1769–1853) composed another to the tune "Belmont" for use with Rous's version.

Since then many notable revisions and translations have occurred: as revised text by James Montgomery in *Songs of Zion* in 1822; as an alternate tune by Thomas Koschat in 1862; as the rendition "Good Shepherd" by Joseph Barnby; as "Crimond" in 1872 by Jessie Seymour Irvine; as "Evan" in 1847 by William Havergal and arranged by Lowell Mason in 1850; as "Martyrdom" in 1800 by Hugh Wilson and arranged by Ralph E. Hudson around 1885.

In every version of the song a single idea radiates: The Lord is a personal shepherd to whomever calls on Him, regarding any need.

With the Lord as your Shepherd you
   have all that you need,
For if you follow in His footsteps
   wherever He may lead,
He will guard and guide and keep you
   in His loving, watchful care,
And when traveling in dark valleys,
   your Shepherd will be there.
His goodness is unfailing, His kind-
   ness knows no end,
For the Lord is a good Shepherd on
   whom you can depend.
So, when your heart is troubled, you'll
   find quiet peace and calm
If you open up the Bible and just read
   this treasured Psalm.

THE LORD'S PRAYER

Our Father, Who art in heaven,
Hallowed be Thy Name.
Thy kingdom come, Thy will be done
On earth as it is in heaven.
Give us this day our daily bread,
And forgive us our debts,
As we forgive our debtors.
And lead us not into temptation,
But deliver us from evil,
For Thine is the Kingdom, and the Power and the Glory forever,
Amen.

How the Hymn Came to Be

The hymn "The Lord's Prayer," also identified as "The Our Father" or "The Pater Noster," is based on the prayer Christ Himself taught to the apostles. It is simultaneously a prayer of praise, penitence, and petition. As a musical prayer of perfect and unselfish love, the text comes from Jesus Himself, as recorded in Matthew 6:9–13.

The music, "Gregorian," by Lowell Mason in 1841, is written as a Gregorian chant, but the hymn is most commonly known by the music Albert Hay Malotte (1895–1964) wrote.

Our Father, who art in heaven,
    hear this little prayer
And reach across the miles today
    that stretch from here to there
So I may feel much closer
    to those I'm fondest of,
And they may know I think of them
    with thankfulness and love.
And help all people everywhere
    who must often dwell apart
To know that they're together
    in the haven of the heart.

THE OLD RUGGED CROSS

On a hill far away stood an old rugged cross,
the emblem of suffering and shame;
And I love that old cross where the dearest and best
for a world of lost sinners was slain.

Refrain: So I'll cherish the old rugged cross,
Till my trophies at last I lay down;
I will cling to the old rugged cross,
And exchange it someday for a crown.

How the Hymn Came to Be

While wrestling with a problem, thirty-year-old George Bennard meditated on Philippians 3:10; not only did its words answer his immediate dilemma, they inspired him to write "The Old Rugged Cross." In January of 1913 Bennard introduced his partially written hymn at a revival meeting.

Bennard and his wife worked tirelessly to organize evangelistic services for more than sixty years. They eventually became officers in the Salvation Army, before George was ordained in the Methodist Episcopal Church.

Bennard died at eighty-five, and a twelve-foot cross stands where he lived the last years of his life, near Reed City, Michigan. Like the song for which the man is remembered, the cross is roughly hewn and rugged—a testament to a beautiful Savior.

Oh, spare me all trouble and save me
   from sorrow,
May each happy day bring
   a brighter tomorrow.
May I never know pain or taste
   bitter woe,
Sadness and suffering I care not to know.
But if I should meet Him sometime face
   to face,
Will I feel oddly strange and a bit out
   of place,
When I look at the marks where the
   nails went in
As He hung on the cross to save us
   from sin?
Will He think me unworthy to be one
   of His own
And too weak and untried to sit at
   His throne?
Will I forfeit my right to a crown set
   with stars,
Because I can show Him no battle scars?
Will the one who suffered and wept
   with pain
Be the one He will welcome to share
   His domain?
Will the trials of life make a crown
   of stars
Unfit to be worn by one without scars?

THERE SHALL BE SHOWERS OF BLESSING

There shall be showers of blessing:
This is the promise of love;
There shall be seasons refreshing,
Sent from the Savior above.

Refrain: Showers of blessing,
Showers of blessing we need:
Mercy drops 'round us are falling,
But for the showers we plead.

How the Hymn Came to Be

During the Civil War, Daniel Webster Whittle (1840–1901) was serving as a major in the Northern Army when he was wounded at the Battle of Vicksburg. While hospitalized he read the New Testament daily. Still he had not accepted Christ as Savior. One night an orderly awakened the major requesting his assistance with a dying youth. At first Whittle hesitated to read and pray over the young man but finally relented. As Whittle prayed for the young soldier, he also prayed for forgiveness of his own faults. With renewed belief in Christ, Whittle later recalled he was showered with blessings.

After the war, Whittle became treasurer of the Elgin Watch Company but within ten years entered the field of evangelism. James McGranahan (1849–1907), a devoted friend of talented musician Philip Bliss, composed the music for Whittle's words.

Each day there are showers of blessings
   sent from the Father above,
For God is a great, lavish giver;
   and there is no end to His love.
And His grace is more than sufficient, His
   mercy is boundless and deep,
And His infinite blessings are countless —
   and all this we're given to keep
If we but seek God and find Him
   and ask for a bounteous measure
Of this wholly immeasurable offering from
   God's inexhaustible treasure.
For no matter how big our dreams are,
   God's blessings are infinitely more,
For always God's giving is greater
   than what we are asking for.

Helen Steiner Rice

'Tis So Sweet to Trust in Jesus

'Tis so sweet to trust in Jesus, just to take Him at His word,
Just to rest upon his promise, just to know, "Thus saith the Lord."

Refrain: Jesus, Jesus, how I trust Him! How I've proved Him o'er and o'er!
Jesus, Jesus, precious Jesus! O for grace to trust Him more!

How the Hymn Came to Be

Louisa M. Rouser (1850–1917) was born in Dover, England. From early childhood, she desired to be a missionary. In 1871 she traveled to America to pursue her goal.

Love has a way of altering plans, and on October 4, 1873, Louisa married. She and her husband moved east, where eventually daughter Lily was born. One day when Lily was four, while the Steads were enjoying a day at the beach, they heard a young boy in the water cry for help. Mr. Stead swam out to rescue the lad but both he and the boy drowned. An act of courageous kindness and heroism turned into a double tragedy.

As time went on and circumstances became bleak for Louisa and Lily, food and money were secretly placed on their doorstep. Those acts of kindness led Louisa to write "'Tis So Sweet to Trust in Jesus." Sometime later mother and daughter departed for South Africa to become missionaries. After ten years of service, Louisa remarried.

The music for "'Tis So Sweet to Trust in Jesus" was composed by William James Kirkpatrick (1838–1921), a talented violinist and cellist.

Whatever our problems, troubles
    and sorrows,
If we trust in the Lord, there'll be
    brighter tomorrows
For there's nothing too much for
    the great God to do,
And all that He asks or expects from you
Is faith that's unshaken by tribulations
    and tears,
That keeps growing stronger along
    with the years,
Content in the knowledge that God
    knows best
And that trouble and sorrow are only
    a test,
For without God's testing of the soul
It never would reach its ultimate goal.
So keep on believing, whatever betide you,
Knowing that God will be with you to
    guide you
And all that He promised will be yours
    to receive
If you trust Him completely and
    always believe.

TO GOD BE THE GLORY

To God be the glory—great things He hath done!
So loved He the world that He gave us His Son,
Who yielded His life an atonement for sin
And opened the Lifegate that all may go in.

Refrain: Praise the Lord, praise the Lord,
Let the earth hear His voice!
Praise the Lord, praise the Lord,
Let the people rejoice!
O come to the Father, through Jesus the Son,
And give Him the glory—great things He has done.

How the Hymn Came to Be

Although "To God Be the Glory" was published in 1875, it remained virtually unknown in the United States until 1954. That's when Cliff Barrows led this song of praise—written by Fanny Crosby (1820–1915)—at a Billy Graham Crusade in Nashville, Tennessee.

Crosby penned hymns as an effort to praise God for His grace and plan for her life. She was so convicted of this idea that she even praised God for her blindness, explaining that it afforded her more time to meditate on His blessings.

The tune "To God Be the Glory" was composed by William H. Doane (1832–1915), who often worked with Crosby, combining his sacred melodies with her inspiring words.

The wonder and glory of the first
    Easter morn,
Like the first Christmas night when the
    Savior was born,
Are blended together in symphonic
    splendor
And God, with a voice that is gentle
    and tender,
Speaks to all hearts attuned to
    His voice,
Bidding His listeners to gladly rejoice.
For He who was born to be crucified
Arose from the grave to be glorified.
And the birds in the trees and the flowers
    of spring
All join in proclaiming this
    heavenly King.

WE HAVE THIS MOMENT TODAY

Hold tight to the sound of the music we're living—
Happy songs from the laughter of children at play;
Hold my hand as we run through the sweet, fragrant meadows,
Making memories of what was today.

Refrain: We have this moment to hold in our hands,
And touch as it slips through our fingers like sand;
Yesterday's gone and tomorrow may never come,
But we have this moment today.

How the Hymn Came to Be

Gloria Gaither was sifting through a box of treasured letters one afternoon in 1975 when the idea for this hymn struck her. What a beautiful "historical paper quilt," she thought, when notes, cards, letters, and other mementos are laid out and stitched together with fond memory, tenderness, and love.

In the nostalgia and cherished reverie she realized how lovely it is to take time to enjoy all the large and small moments of every day. Memories, she sings in this beloved hymn, live forever!

Yesterday's dead, tomorrow's unborn,
So there's nothing to fear and nothing
   to mourn,
For all that is past and all that has been
Can never return to be lived once again.
And what lies ahead or the things
   that will be
Are still in God's hands, so it is not
   up to me
To live in the future that is God's
   great unknown,
For the past and the present God claims
   for His own.
So all I need do is to live for today
And trust God to show me the truth
   and the way,
For it's only the memory of things
   that have been
And expecting tomorrow to bring
   trouble again
That fills my today, which God
   wants to bless,
With uncertain fears and borrowed distress.
For all I need live for is this one
   little minute,
For life's here and now and eternity's in it.

WHAT A FRIEND WE HAVE IN JESUS

What a Friend we have in Jesus, all our sins and griefs to bear!
What a privilege to carry everything to God in prayer!
O what peace we often forfeit, O what needless pain we bear,
All because we do not carry everything to God in prayer!

How the Hymn Came to Be

Joseph Scriven (1819–1886), learned early in life to give his sorrows to the Lord. On the eve of his wedding day, his bride-to-be drowned. Departing his homeland of Ireland, he sailed to Port Hope, Canada, in search of a fresh life. At age thirty-six Scriven found a new love and became engaged, but—unbelievable as it may seem—prior to the wedding his fiancée died suddenly!

Though Joseph Scriven suffered many trials, he found Jesus to be his best friend and resolved to devote his life to "being a friend" to others. In 1857 he wrote the poem "What a Friend We Have in Jesus" as an encouragement for his ailing mother in Ireland. It was never his intention that it be made public. A copy was found by a colleague and published in an 1869 collection of poems created by Scriven. In 1886 at age seventy-seven, death came to this "Good Samaritan of Port Hope" through an accidental drowning.

The tune used with this poem is "Erie" by Charles C. Converse, a German-American lawyer and composer, who by chance had read the collection of Scriven's poems. The combination of text and tune has endured for generations.

God is no stranger in a faraway place —
He's as close as the wind that blows 'cross
   my face.
It's true I can't see the wind as it blows,
But I feel it around me and my heart
   surely knows
That God's mighty hand can be
   felt everywhere,
For there's nothing on earth that is not
   in God's care.
The sky and the stars,
   the waves and the sea,
The dew on the grass,
   the leaves on a tree
Are constant reminders of God
   and His nearness,
Proclaiming His presence
   with crystal-like clearness . . .
So how could I think God was
   far, far away
When I feel Him beside me every hour
   of the day?
And I've plenty of reasons to know God's
   my Friend,
And this is one friendship that time
   cannot end.

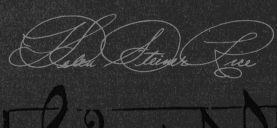

WHEN I SURVEY THE WONDROUS CROSS

When I survey the wondrous cross
On which the Prince of Glory died,
My richest gain I count but loss,
And pour contempt on all my pride.

O GOD, OUR HELP IN AGES PAST

O God, our help in ages past,
Our hope for years to come,
Our shelter from the stormy blast,
And our eternal home.

How the Hymns Came to Be

Isaac Watts (1674–1748) wrote "When I Survey the Wondrous Cross" to help people reflect not only on the death of Jesus on the cross but also the love that drew him there. Serving as pastor of a Reformed church in London, Watts advocated a transformation in congregational singing and moved to base hymn texts more on personal feelings.

In 1824, seventy-six years after Watts's death, his hymn "When I Survey the Wondrous Cross" was put to the tune "Hamburg," based on a Gregorian Chant, so named in honor of Pope Gregory, one of the earliest church leaders to recognize the need for improving church music. "Hamburg" was arranged by Lowell Mason (1792–1872), the first music teacher in an American public school and credited with creating more than 1,600 religious compositions.

Watts is often referred to as "the father of English hymn writing." He composed more than six hundred hymns in his lifetime, including "O God, Our Help in Ages Past," the title of which came about when another hymn writer, John Wesley, altered the original "Our God, Our Help."

God, how little I was really aware
Of the pain and the trouble
    and deep despair
That flood the hearts of those in pain
As they struggle to cope but feel it's in vain.
Crushed with frustration and
    with no haven to seek,
With broken spirits and bodies so weak —
And yet they forget Christ suffered and died
And hung on the cross and was crucified —
And He did it all so some happy day
When the sorrows of earth
    have all passed away,
We who have suffered will forever be free
To live with God in eternity.

YOU FILL THE DAY

Run with your head up in the wind
Run with your head up in the wind, the wind
Your head high, your soul an open door,
And breathe the wind that makes you free
And breathe the wind that makes you free

Refrain: You fill the day with Your glory and Your power
You fill the night with Your quiet and Your deep love

How the Hymn Came to Be

Artist and composer Joe Wise had just finished reading Edward Scillebeeckx' *Christ the Sacrament of the Encounter with God* one day when this hymn came to him.

"I was especially enamored with and engaged in nature," he explains. "I discovered it as a path for a sacrament to God—direct, and available to everyone, access to God, and a way to dispel our separation. The song flowed right out of my pen and out of my experience in the rain while out in a field."

I come to meet You, God, and as
    I linger here
I seem to feel You very near.
A rustling leaf, a rolling slope
Speak to my heart of endless hope.
The sun just rising in the sky,
The waking birdlings as they fly,
The grass all wet with morning dew
Are telling me I just met You.
And, gently, thus the day is born
As night gives way to breaking morn,
And once again I've met You, God,
And worshipped on Your holy sod.
For who could see the dawn break through
Without a glimpse of heaven and You?
For who but God could make the day
And softly put the night away?

ACKNOWLEDGMENTS

*S*incere appreciation is hereby expressed to our loving Creator for designing the melodious symphony of life and the bestowal of talents; to Dorothy C. Lingg, Helen Steiner Rice™ Foundation office manager for unlimited dependability and meticulous assistance; Ruth Stafford Peal for graciously providing the foreword; Jeanette Thomason and Mary Wenger for sensitive editing; composers of lyrics and music; copyright holders and publishers for gracious permissions; the CD participants for sharing their God-given talents in a generous manner; narrator, musicians, music directors, members of church choirs, accompanists, soloists, recording technicians, sound engineer, and all who contributed in any way.

An enormous round of applause and gratitude to the trustees of the Helen Steiner Rice™ Foundation for supporting this project, thus enabling the CD to be included as a gift. This CD is a gift from the Helen Steiner Rice™ Foundation to purchasers of the book *Awake My Soul and Sing*.

Special acknowledgment is given to:

Virginia R. Wiltse, narrator
The Allen Temple A.M.E. Church combined choirs under the direction of Robert Gazaway
Choir of Christ Church Cathedral, Ernie Hoffman, organist and director of music
St. Antoninus/St. Joseph's Gathering Choral Society, soloist Mary Jo Katona, director Wylie Howell
Hamilton County Sheriff's Pipes & Drums, Cincinnati, Ohio, Stephen Watt
Hyde Park Community United Methodist Church, Neal V. Hamlin, choirmaster and director of music
Adele Gratsch Lippert, soprano soloist
Maurice Mandell, bass and Louise Mandell, mezzo-soprano, soloists
Shiloh United Methodist Chancel choir, Jerry W. Suit, director of music
St. Ignatius Celebrate, Lisa Pollard Hasselbeck (12-string guitar), Robert Imhoff (electric bass), Karen Gilbert Gately (flute), Pam Johnson Rosenacker (keyboard and strings), Jenny Sedler Bates (vocalist), Mary Sedler Massa (vocalist), Roger Klug (electric bass on "Surely the Presence of the Lord")
St. John's Westminster Union Church choir and soloists, Paula Jordan and Larry Findlay; Laura Backley-Bolduc, director; Josh Nemith, accompanist
Roger Klug, sound engineer

poco cresc.